Introduction

Unlike other books on leadership, this one is designed to be used by individuals at <u>all</u> levels of leadership or management. For the novice, this book will be an indispensable introductory text. For the more experienced, it will serve as a powerful resource to refresh, inspire and innovate. For both, this book will provide easily applicable concepts to help shape, define and lead an organization.

The contents in this book are designed to be an easy, quick and practical resource that exposes you to a variety of theories, quotes, concepts, anecdotes, and ideas – each of which will provide substantive insight into how to be a more effective and focused leader. A notes section is included at the end of this book as well. I strongly encourage you utilize it to write down your thoughts, ideas and inspirations.

Let's get started!

"Keep your fears to yourself, but share your courage with others."

— *Robert Louis Stevenson*

Trait Leadership

Based on the "Great Man" Theory (Carlyle, 1840), Trait Leadership focuses on defining the "universal qualities" - or traits - that all leaders supposedly share. It argues that successful leaders differ from others by possessing core personality traits that contribute to their successful leadership. The trait approach identifies physiological, intellectual, task-related, and social characteristics, such as:

- **Achievement drive**: High level of effort, high levels of ambition, energy and initiative
- **Leadership motivation:** an intense desire to lead others to reach shared goals
- **Honesty and integrity**: trustworthy, reliable, and open
- **Self-confidence**: Belief in one's self, ideas, and ability
- **Cognitive ability**: Capable of exercising good judgment, strong analytical abilities, and conceptually skilled
- **Knowledge of business**: Knowledge of industry and other technical matters
- **Emotional Maturity**: well adjusted, does not suffer from severe psychological disorders.
- **Others**: charisma, creativity and flexibility

Framing Theory in Organizations

Framing is a type of communication designed to get others to accept one meaning over another. Furthermore, it seeks to guide how organizational members understand and respond to their professional environment. It's a skill many successful leaders possess, yet one that is not often taught. Frames are abstract notions that serve to help organize/structure social meaning. The avenues for "framing" particular situations are:

- Metaphor: giving an idea/program a new meaning by comparing it to something else.

- Stories, myths and legends.

- Traditions, rituals and ceremonies.

- Slogans, jargon and catchphrases.

- Artifacts: illuminate values through physical objects.

- Contrast: describing a subject in terms of what it is not.

- Spin: talking about a concept so as to give it a positive or negative connotation.

Organizational Communication: A Competency Approach

The communication competency approach views communication as an organic system comprised of several parts. This is very important for many organizations because the *type* of communication within the organization is a direct by-product of the *culture and norms* of the organization. In short, an organization with unclear values/norms will often have unclear objectives and unclear communication. Leaders need to ensure that their employees are "competent" in their communication – not just in *what* they say, but the *means* by which they *send and receive* information.

Knowledge competency: Ability to understand the organizational communication environment.

Sensitivity competency: Ability to sense organizational meanings and feelings accurately.

Skills competency: Ability to analyze organizational situations accurately and to initiate and consume organizational messages effectively.

Values competency: Importance of taking responsibility for effective communication, thereby contributing to organizational success.

One of my earliest leadership positions was working as an operations director for a post-production facility in Los Angeles, CA. I enjoyed the job and was fortunate enough to have excellent employees as well as upper management that was responsive and innovative. The hours were long and the variety of projects ensured that there were very few boring days. In our weekly management meeting, the CEO decided that it would be a great idea to buy all the employees lunch every Friday. All of the managers, including myself, quickly agreed that is was a great idea....Wrong!

Lunch orders for 30+ people is difficult enough as it is. Combine that with the fact that it was a 24 hour facility, which meant that almost half the employees wouldn't benefit because they worked the night shift – I'm not sure what we we're thinking. Furthermore, we became quickly aware of how picky many employees were, specific dietary restrictions, etc. In short, the issue of lunch became the *primary concern* for many employees the first thing Friday morning! My office was inundated with lunch request, complaints, cajoling and reminders that "We had Chinese last week!" Inevitably, we had many who were unhappy with their free lunch. Ironically, in our effort to make them happier, we managed to do *the exact opposite*. I learned an important lesson that I would like to pass on. Yes, it is important to reward employees – however – the rewards should have *few variables* and involve *as little input from employees as possible*. In short, your rewards should be standardized and universally applied. Once you open the door to allowing employees a choice into how they will be rewarded, you have opened the door to a world of trouble.

Knowing Your Corporate Culture

A leader must be able to accurately assess whether their organization tends to be risk-averse, adventurous, or a combination of both.

Risk-Averse:

- New ideas are often dismissed.
- Organization is not always driven by external needs.
- Emphasis within the organization is on dealing with problems.
- Stability/experience are the most valued attributes of the organization.
- The good of the company is put before the individual.
- Command/control are the dominant processes.
- Difficult to change the corporate mind-set.

Adventurous:

- New/creative ideas are welcomed.
- Focus is mainly on the needs of the customer.
- Emphasis on taking advantage of new opportunities.
- Motivation/innovation are the most valued attributes of the organization.
- Corporate and individual aims are largely aligned.
- Staff are allowed autonomy and are able to show initiative.
- Policies and ideas are frequently changed, according to circumstances.

Remember, that neither culture is "right" or "wrong." However, once you understand your organizational culture better, you can be well-prepared to steer your organization toward the goals you want and be able to better manage problems when they arise.

"If ignorant both of your enemy and yourself, you are certain to be in peril."

- Sun Tzu

"Don't tell people how to do things, tell them what to do and let them surprise you with their results."

- George Patton

Preparing to Lead

Leading people can often be difficult because…well, they're people, with with all their faults, foibles, strengths, weakness, likes and dislikes. As a leader, you shouldn't waste time worrying about these, because it is extremely unlikely that you will be able to change these personality characteristics. Instead, before you step into any leadership role – you must ask yourself some key questions.

1) *What* are we trying to achieve?
2) In what *ways* are we trying to achieve it?
3) What *major* issues do we face?
4) What do *others* think of the organization – good and bad?
5) Are we properly *organized* to achieve what we want in the way we want?

As you can see, I've italicized certain words above to guide you in being more specific about the goals and challenges that are before you. A goal that is not specific is nothing more than an aspiration, desire or want. For example, "Making more money" is not a goal, but "increasing revenue by 18% by the end of next quarter" is a goal. Leaders do not aspire or want – they achieve. Therefore, before you consider taking any leadership role, in any capacity, you need to be able to answer the above questions as <u>specifically</u> as possible. I have seen many leaders and organizations fail because they were unable to see clearly the real issues but were instead caught up in minutia. As a leader, answering these questions will create a coherent, well-focused plan that your employees can get behind.

Managing Meetings

In case you haven't noticed already, this book is very no-frills. Not a lot of fancy diagrams, bright colors or flourishes. Why? <u>Because it serves no purpose</u>. Just like 95% of the meetings that happen in organizations. Very little, if anything, is truly decided in a meeting. Most of the time, they're gatherings for people to air their opinions before the decision is made somewhere else, or by someone else. Sometimes the decision has already been made and the meeting is a pretense to give the illusion that other voices are being heard.

One of the major complaints that I hear from both employees and managers is the amount of time wasted in meetings. This is very true, because real leaders have very few meetings. Why? Because they have already done the groundwork of creating a strong organizational culture with clear expectations, values, goals and norms. The rare meeting is usually because something amazingly good or catastrophically bad has happened. However, inevitably, there will be a reason for a meeting. Therefore, it is your responsibility to make it as productive and efficient as possible by keeping these thoughts in mind:

- Always be clear about the purpose of the meeting.
- If an issue can be resolved without a meeting, cancel it.
- Is there a better, alternate way of addressing the issue without a meeting?
- Only invite the relevant people, with the appropriate authority or expertise, to the meeting.
- Does everyone need to stay the entire time?
- Start meeting by reinforcing objectives/goals and close meeting with the same reinforcement.

The Role of Strategy

It's not enough for a company to have a successful product or service, they must have a strategy. "Strategy" is a process that enables an organization to achieve results. It's also about understanding what your organization does and being able to have a long-term vision of what you want the organization to become. While "strategic plans" can vary depending on your goals, they generally contain the following components:

Direction Statement
- Mission Statement (your purpose)
- Company Vision Statement (your desired future)
- Company's business definition (what you do)
- Competitive advantages (where you are better than competitors)
- Core competencies (tangible & intangible assets)
- Values (beliefs that define the company culture)

Strategic Objectives
- Key Result Areas (KRA)
- Measurements for KRA
- Objectives to meet KRA

Priority Issues
- Competitive concerns
- Where can you add/create value for customers or clients?
- Expansion, technology, acquisitions, etc.

Action Plans
- Strategic initiatives
- Measurement of success/failure - specific metrics or time frames
- Resources required
- Anticipated cost and gain

How to Create a Culture

As a leader, creating an effective, supportive, innovative and dynamic culture is of utmost importance. Culture creates an identity for your organization, for both employees and customers. When you think of Fed-Ex what comes to mind? Apple? Coca-Cola? None of these companies started with a culture or identity – they were created. They were created by being very clear about their values, norms, goals and beliefs. How can leaders create a strong organizational culture?

Example setting: What do you pay attention to? How do you respond to a crisis? How do you deal with disagreement? How do you treat others around you?

Storytelling: What stories do you tell about your successes or failures? What stories do you tell about customers or clients? Do you tell stories about serving customers or how to avoid upsetting them?

Education & Artifacts: What type of symbols represent your organization? How is time managed? How are employees expected to address each other?

These are just a few, very simple, ways that leaders can help to implement and create an organizational culture. However, culture is something that must be attended to and monitored until it becomes deeply ingrained. If employees can buy into you, they will buy into your culture – and vice versa.

Theory X and Theory Y

In the 1960s, MIT management professor Douglas McGregor developed a theory to address the issues of employee motivation in his book, *The Human Side of Enterprise,* which has cast a profound and influential shadow on management theory. McGregor argues that there are two, fundamental types of motivational frameworks, each overseen by a particular "type" of manager.

Theory X
Employees are seen as inherently lazy and unmotivated, therefore an authoritarian style of management is needed in order to fulfill objectives. A strongly defined hierarchy and strict measures of control are needed at every level. According to Theory X, employee motivation is largely enhanced by tangible, extrinsic rewards or threats of punishment. Theory X managers often seek to find individuals who are responsible for failures or successes and assign individual blame or reward as opposed to collective, group success.

Theory Y
Employees are assumed to be naturally ambitious, seek to be creative, and are self-motivated. It is believed that employees can enjoy their work and find intrinsic rewards in their jobs. Theory Y managers believe that given the right conditions, employees will be self-directed and will want to be efficient and productive. Theory Y managers also value employee development and encourage open lines of communication with subordinates.

"A leader...is like a shepherd. He stays behind the flock, letting the most nimble go out ahead, whereupon the others follow, not realizing that all along they are being directed from behind."

- Nelson Mandela

"You don't lead by pointing and telling people some place to go. You lead by going to that place and making a case."

– Ken Kesey

On October 30th, 1863 an article appeared in the *New York Times* recounting President Abraham Lincoln's response to the many complaints and criticisms that General Ulysses S. Grant was imbibing too frequently and was largely considered by many others to be a "drunkard."

When someone charged Gen. Grant, in the President's hearing, with drinking too much liquor, Mr. Lincoln, recalling Gen. Grant's successes, said that if he could find out what brand of whisky Grant drank, he would send a barrel of it to all the other commanders.

President Lincoln understood one of the most important things about effective leadership:

When you have good employees, stay out of their way.

Know Your Goals

All leaders need to have goals. However, you also need to know what *type* of goal you are looking to achieve. In doing so, the chances for your success increase dramatically. Goals can be broken down in to three types:

Outcome goals: These represent the point of the enterprise or your effort. These are goals that we can recognize by a definable, quantitative success such as winning a contract, finishing a marathon, or shipping a product by a certain date.

Process goals: These are the "how" goals. They focus on the behaviors that will bring the outcome goal to fruition. These types of goals are based on action or activity goals that will enable us to be successful. For example, finishing a marathon (outcome goal) will require daily, consistent training (process goal).

Learning goals: These are goals to acquire knowledge or skills. These may be necessary if we lack the knowledge or expertise to accomplish outcome and process goals. While it's not always necessary to master learning goals before we move onto process or outcome goals. However, if done, the length of time to completion and the likelihood of setbacks and frustrations will be greatly decreased.

Two monks were returning to the monastery in the evening. It had rained and there were puddles of water on the road sides. At one place a beautiful young woman was standing, unable to walk across because of a puddle of water. The elder monk went to her, lifted her and carried her to the other side of the road, and continued his way to the monastery. In the evening the younger monk came to the elder monk and said, "Sir, as monks, we cannot touch a woman?" The elder monk answered, "Yes, brother. That is true." Then the younger monk asks again, "but then Sir, how is that you lifted that woman on the roadside?" The elder monk smiled at him and told him, "I left her on the other side of the road, but you are still carrying her."

*****

Often, especially when discussing leadership, we're constantly told about the importance of having a "vision," being "forward thinking" or constantly think about the future. However, what is equally important, and often overlooked, is how necessary it is for an effective leader to be "present." This means that dwelling on mistakes or being too focused on future probabilities can often blind us to what needs to be done <u>now</u>. Many leaders have been derailed by consistently drowning in the "what ifs," "should haves" and the "could happen" of the organization. When we are too busy looking forward or backwards, we are not "present." A leader who is not "present" in the moment is a leader who is distracted. A leader who is distracted is a leader that fails.

Functional Leadership

The functional approach to leadership argues that leaders exist to perform essential functions or behaviors that help organizations be successful. Unlike "trait leadership" which emphasizes *personal* characteristics and qualities, functional leadership separates leadership *behaviors* into two categories:

1) **Task functions**: focused on getting the job or project done. Whether appointed or elected, the leader's primary focus is to ensure that the end goal is met. Often accomplished by organizing structural elements such as:

   -Setting agendas
   -Recording what is completed
   -Determining meeting times
   -Distributing information
   -Evaluating ideas

2) **Process functions**: Responsible for maintaining a harmonious environment and encouraging an amiable climate within the group. Focused on listening and responding to others as well as managing relationships through:

   -Encouraging reticent members to talk
   -Mediating conflict
   -Compromising or helping others to compromise
   -Gatekeeping and ensuring participation

These two functional approaches are not mutually exclusive, as a leader can embrace and excel in both areas. Experiment with the functional approach and see what works best for you.

Hiring

Too often we spend time outwardly focusing on some imaginary "perfect candidate" that will solve all our problems. Of course we'll will recognize the "perfect" person when we see them, right? However, before you focus outward, you need to look inward to your organization and have a very clear idea of who you are and what you do – not what you "wished" you were or "hope" to be. If you get the right people first, training them easy. You need to understand *your* organization's skill set and what is required for an employee to thrive in your *particular* organization.

Hard skills: Job skills that are absolutely necessary for a candidate to have. These are baseline requirements and you do not have the time to train the employee, but can use them to enhance and develop the employee.

Soft skills: Critical to functioning in the interpersonal environment and operating as a team player. They also include intangibles such as adaptability, ability to communicate with others, problem solving and self-discipline.

Behaviors: Personal characteristics or presentation of self, such as punctuality, neatness, courtesy or pleasant attitude.

Goals: What you expect the employee to accomplish. The specific tasks or mastery will you expect them to exhibit in your workplace.

So remember, before you interview potential employees, interview yourself.

"If you want to build a ship, don't drum up the men to gather wood, divide the work, and give orders. Instead, teach them to yearn for the vast and endless sea."

- Antoine de Saint-Exupéry

"When you put together deep knowledge about a subject that intensely matters to you, charisma happens. You gain courage to share your passion, and when you do that, folks follow."

- Jerry Porras

Workplace Conflict

When conflict arises in the workplace, it's very important for a leader to maintain their composure and ensure that all parties, within reason, are treated as fairly as possible. It's important for leaders to understand the "nature" of the conflict process to avoid overacting or not reacting effectively enough. Management scholar Louis Pondy, in his work, *Organizational Conflict: Concepts and Models,"* identifies five phases of conflict:

Latent conflict: When two or more parties value the same limited resources (time, office space, expense budget, etc.) This type of conflict is predicated on the human desire have what others have or to be treated equitably.

Perceived conflict: Not overt, but potential problems are perceived and sensed by at least one member. At this point negative attribution is taking place (i.e. Mark gets the corner office because he's a "brown noser" who rats other people out to the boss).

Felt conflict: The conflict is personalized, emotions become involved and the aggrieved party begins to consider how to address it. As this consideration continues, emotional escalation is likely.

Manifest conflict: When the conflict becomes overt and one or both parties express the conflict and attempt to resolve it through confrontation, bargaining, or problem-solving.

Conflict aftermath: Can be short-term or long-term. Participants experience the consequences of the conflict, not only in specific agreements/arrangements but for relationships, identities, and organizational or group culture.

Power and Leadership

There's a reason the phrase, "Heavy is the head that wears the crown" is still a relevant. Before you can apply power effectively, you must understandd what it is and how it's utilized.

Legitimate: Bestowed by the organization through various, legitimate means. For example, being hired as a manger or CEO.

Reward: Ability to grant rewards to employees or subordinates, such as raises, bonuses, etc. Often tied to legitimate power, but is not always the case. A manager may have the ability or decision capacity to reward, but the *approval* may have to come from someone above them.

Coercive: Ability to force others to do something or punish. It derives from the organization's hierarchy and is usually a sanctioned action. Can be minimal, such as docking someone's pay or more severe, such as termination.

Expert: The result of accrued knowledge, expertise or experience. The more specialized the knowledge is, the more potential power is available. Furthermore, the scarcity of the knowledge can create a large resource of power for the individual that has it.

Referent: Gained through the respect and admiration of others. This is an earned power that increases over time. It can be developed through other forms of power, but the overuse of coercive power or reward can greatly diminish it.

You should always be honest with yourself about your type of power and where it comes from. Trust me, your employees already know.

Becoming a Magnet

Finding good employees is easy...if you can be the place that good employees seek out. How do you attract the best people? You have to recognize that they are not just meeting *your* needs, but that you're meeting *their* needs as well. There are some core "needs" that all employees seek.

Safety: Physical safety, emotional safety or working for a business that is "too big to fail." For others, it might be the opportunity to develop or hone transferable skills. You must communicate that the position is stable, consistent and can provide personal/professional growth

Risk: Employees are often okay with risk, but what they avoid is unquantifiable risk. Would you feel more comfortable skydiving if: (1) you knew parachutes opened correctly 95% of the time or (2) no one had any idea/data to tell you how often parachutes opened correctly? People are fine with taking risk, if they feel they have the information to manage it, some sense of control and can see the potential rewards. Acknowledge the risk and tell potential employees how you will help them manage it, and explain the payoff.

Growth & Variety: People seek to learn new skills, develop their talents, and increase the variety of their tasks. However, variety is not enough. You must explain how they will be vital and integral to the functioning and success of the organization. How will their involvement benefit the organization?

Community: It's far more attractive to be part of a bigger vision and connected to others with goals that supersede a paycheck. If you just want them to make money for the company, hire a temp worker. If you want them to stay, even if they get a better financial offer, make them part of something bigger than themselves.

A young, very earnest Zen student approached his teacher, and asked, "If I work very hard and remain diligent how long will it take for me to find Zen?" The Master thought about this, then replied, "Ten years." The student then said, "But what if I work very, very hard and really apply myself to learn fast -- How long then?" The Master replied, "Well, twenty years." Still, the student persisted, "But, if I really, really work at it. How long then?" "Thirty years," replied the Master. "But, I do not understand," said the disappointed student. "Each time that I say I will work harder, you say it will take me longer. Why do you say that?" The Master replied, "When you have one eye on the goal, you only have one eye on the path."

*****

If you're reading this book, most likely and you have lived, grown up, and worked in the American culture. Deadlines, quick fixes and immediate results. We have multi-billion dollar industries dedicated to keeping us obsessed fighting a foe that will **never** be defeated: the inevitable march of time and decline of our bodies. As a leader, your time is transitory. When you focus too much on how "quickly" you can get something done, you <u>will</u> begin to take shortcuts. It becomes very easy to cut corners ethically and financially. It begins to make sense to cut corners with your personal or professional relationships. Do not be consumed with quickness, be consumed with process, integrity and consistency. Your customers and employees will notice.

Strategic Planning: 5 Steps

The strategic plan is the primary tool to align an organizational goals and ensure effective execution of strategy. "Strategic plans" can vary, but every plan should address some fundamental concepts:

1. **Analysis of external and internal factors, such as:**
   Market trends
   Impending/changing technology
   Impending/changing legislation
   Alliances and partnerships with outside firms
   Organizational culture/finances
   Company processes

2. **SWOT Analysis**
   Strengths: capabilities that need to be leveraged
   Weaknesses: qualities that inhibit growth and success
   Opportunities: trends and forces that can be capitalized on
   Threats: events or forces, outside of your control, that you must mitigate

3. **Priority Issues**
   Areas that should be focused on for the long term
   Strengths to be increased & weaknesses to be fixed

4. **Action Plans**
   Detail the objectives, tasks, etc. for carrying out the priority issues

5. **Finalize the Plan**
   Write corporate direction statement
   Clarify the objectives
   Summarize the overarching initiatives

"**Leadership is the capacity to translate vision into reality.**"

-Warren Bennis

"My own definition of leadership is this: The capacity and the will to rally men and women to a common purpose and the character which inspires confidence."

– General Bernard Montgomery

Be water, my friend

Bruce Lee was not only the greatest martial artists who ever lived but he was also an astute philosopher and keen student of personal development and achievement. In 1971, at the height of his success, Mr. Lee gave an interview on the *Pierre Berton Show*, in which he was asked to define his personal philosophy:

"Be like water making its way through cracks. Do not be assertive, but adjust to the object, and you shall find a way around or through it. If nothing within you stays rigid, outward things will disclose themselves."

Empty your mind, be formless. Shapeless, like water. If you put water into a cup, it becomes the cup. You put water into a bottle and it becomes the bottle. You put it in a teapot, it becomes the teapot. Now, water can flow or it can crash. Be water, my friend."

Adaptability means being able to, and more importantly, willing to modify yourself when needed. Often times, this is seen as "weak" when it is exactly the opposite. However, only those entities that can effectively react to environmental circumstances and adapt when necessary, will survive. This is the same for any organization or business. The most effective leaders are the ones who can steer their organization with the current and not against it. Also, it's of paramount importance for leaders to be malleable in their thinking. I have met many leaders who are convinced that there is only one way to do "customer service" or only one way to be "efficient." If your leadership thoughts are written in stone, like a rock in the river, it will eventually be worn away by the current.

Great leaders adapt!

Generating Ideas

The true reality is that a leader is only as good as those they lead. While you may have a title or a position above several others, at the end of the day, your success or failure will ultimately depend on those who follow you. Generating good ideas from employees and management are indispensable to great leaders.

Promoting Creativity
Don't allow the pursuit of consensus to kill creative ideas or initiative. Try to flatten the organizational hierarchy and remove blockages to developing ideas. Try and foster an open environment that is not stagnated by concepts or inhibits integration of ideas that aren't internally developed.

Stimulating Ideas
You can't sit around and wait on good ideas to fall out of the sky. Use meetings effectively and insist that everyone come to the meeting with at least two new ideas. Also, ensure that ideas cannot be summarily dismissed without discussion. Encourage expression because even a "bad" idea can often lead to an excellent one, but you'll never know if people are scared to pitch "bad" ideas in the first place.

Brainstorming
Is more than sitting in a room and talking until something miraculously innovative happens. You are looking for *organized creativity*. Analyze the situation and create a shortlist of strong ideas, then have a debate session where assumptions can be challenged and discussed. This is where you are looking to take an idea from conception to fruition.

Communication & Leadership

Almost every leadership book talks about the importance of "effective communication," but few define what it is. To understand communication, in any manner, you have to understand what theoretical/ideological frameworks that it comes from. Aristotle's (384-322 BC) most famous work, *Rhetoric*, provides us with some important insights into the nature of communication as a human activity.

- Communication is "purposive." People communicate with the *specific intention* of affecting or influencing others. Therefore, communication efforts should be evaluated on whether they succeed. If so - how? If not - why not?

- Communication comes in three types: *forensic* oratory is speaking in the courts and/or in an adversary system; *deliberative* oratory is speaking in a group to influence/guide a decision; *epideictic* oratory is speaking during a ceremony or special occasion.

- Persuasion is a result of three types of appeals: *ethos* (credibility), *logos* (logical support/argument) and *pathos* (emotional appeal to the audience).

- "Logical proofs" are an essential part of communication and persuasion. Of these, there are two primary types: *inartistic* (facts, statistics, quantifiable data) and *artistic* (the skill, credibility, and persona of the speaker).

Contextual Intelligence

Leaders with "contextual intelligence" understand the intersection between external events (stock market, political/social unrest, etc.) and their personal choices and leadership strategies. Contextual intelligence is the ability to see the "big-picture" that may force changes and modifications for their organization.

- **Self-knowledge**: understanding and awareness of your values and beliefs. It enables ethical judgments and allows you to predict the impact of your wishes, biases, role models, needs, limitations, strengths, etc. The one things that influences your leadership more than anything is your personal, emotional, moral and psychological makeup. Know yourself before anything else!

- **Social-network knowledge**: the ability to recognize and assess the information coming from other sources (friends, colleagues, etc.). This type of knowledge enables you to understand the subtle signals, tendencies and arguments from others who may be attempting to influence you.

- **Organizational knowledge**: understanding the culture of your organization or business. This can be explicit knowledge, such as mission statements or implicit ones, such as values, norms and behavior.

- **Stakeholder knowledge**: the history, expectations, needs and desires of those who depend on your leadership. This requires an understanding of the central interest of everyone who has a stake in the organization's success. This understanding will enable you to embrace the needs and values to get the trust and commitment of others.

"Trust Melanie"

I'm a big movie fan. One of my favorite movies is *Jackie Brown*, directed by Quentin Tarantino. There is a scene that takes place in a bar between the actors Samuel Jackson (Ordell Robbie) and Robert DeNiro (Louis Gara) that is extremely instructive to those of us that manage and lead others. In this scene, Ordell and Louis discuss the trustworthiness of Ordell's girlfriend, Melanie.

Louis: But – but you trust Melanie around your business?

Ordell: Oh…she tried to play you against me, didn't she?

Louis: Yeah…a little.

Ordell: I knew it. See, you didn't even have to say nothin' I <u>know</u> that woman.

Louis: I don't understand. I don't know why you'd keep someone around your business that you can't even trust.

Ordell: I ain't gotta trust her. I <u>know</u> her.

Louis: I don't know what that means, man.

Ordell: Well…it's like this. You can't trust Melanie, but you can always trust Melanie…to be Melanie.

A good leader knows their employees. A good leaders knows who their "Melanie" is, and more importantly, how to use them effectively if need be.

"The most important thing in communication is hearing what isn't said."

– Peter Drucker

"Effective communication is 20% what you know and 80% how you feel about what you know."

- Jim Rohn

Identifying Resistance

At some point, all organizations will undergo some form of change. Actually, being forced to address change is often a good sign, as it means you're still a viable entity and haven't gone out of business yet. "Resistance" among employees/subordinates can often be amorphous and tough to quantify, let alone address effectively. The primary forms of resistance are:

- Outright defiance.
- Agreement to do something, but failure to follow through.
- Emotional attachment to the way things "used to be done."
- Diminishing commitment to the job.

Resistance can come from ill intent, dissatisfaction or fear of the unknown. How can you overcome this?

- **Information**: Give employees, etc. information about the market forces/environment that is causing the change, and how your strategy will mitigate those forces and benefit the employees.

- **Involvement**: When possible, and as much as is feasible, invite employees to help plan, draft initiatives, develop strategy, etc. This will develop a personal investment for your employees.

- **Coaching**: Identify the reasons for resistance (lack of information, fear, etc.) and look for opportunities to help overcome or correct them.

- **Improvement plan**: Develop a plan with HR, whereby employees will have a clearly defined and objective standard by which they will be evaluated once the change/new policy is implemented.

Organizational Identity

A businesses is just like any living organism, meaning that it:

(1) Must delineate boundaries between itself and its surroundings.

(2) Monitor and maintain those boundaries constantly.

Defining "organizational identity" can be difficult, but it can best be understood as the *central*, *distinct*, and *enduring* dimensions of an organization. What gives an organization a "central" or "unique" identity? First, uniqueness is developed from the perception of differences *between or among* organizations (HBO vs. Showtime, Pepsi vs. Coca-Cola).

Stability is the key to establishing an enduring organizational identity. Your organizational stability will always be assailed by external forces (social, political, psychological, and material), however, these same forces can be *utilized as resources* to develop an enduring corporate/organizational identity.

Your organization's CORE POV (point-of-view) will determine how these external forces will become stories that your organization tells about itself, how employees discuss their work, and the manner in which your organization interacts with the larger world.

An organizational identity is not based on a "mission statement," it's based on the stories/narratives your business, and employees, tell about your successes, and what they mean to you.

Evaluating Performance

Evaluating the "soft skills" of employees is a major challenge for leaders of organizations. While you may have some quantitative, hard data (i.e. sales reports, balance sheets, etc.) on which to make decisions, you are ultimately dealing with people – *and people are not quantitative, hard data*. While the traditional adage that "10% of the salespeople make 90% of the sales" may have some merit, that is not what *grows and develops* a business. To truly grow and develop a business, you must look for "soft skills" that translate into the interpersonal world of business. So, what *qualitative* criteria can we utilize?

The extra mile: Exceeding expectations in accomplishing task/strategic initiatives.

Creativity: Devising novel and fresh ways to accomplish tasks that can be used elsewhere in the organization.

Teamwork: Collaborative skills, ability to self-manage and resolve conflict, and the willingness to share information and talents.

Presentation skills: Ability to get ideas/concepts across quickly to decision makers, clients, etc.

Knowledge & Learning: Employees understand the company's goals, their own roles in supporting strategy and implementing action plans.

Attitudes & Values: Demonstrating the attitudes and values required to achieve the company's strategic objective

Rewarding Results

How companies compensate and reward employees is quite varied. Depending on your position, you might have control over salaries, stock options, bonuses, etc. Conversely, in other companies, management determines compensation for the entire roster of employees and managers have less input in how employees are rewarded financially.

Regardless of the manner or means in which employees are compensated, there is a major <u>emotional/psychological</u> requirement that must be met if you want dedicated, focused employees.

They must <u>understand</u> the system of compensation! Meaning, first and foremost, there must be clarity of both expectations and results. In order to develop a clear, structured "reward" matrix – you must be able to answer the following questions for your employees:

- What exactly is expected of them, and what exactly will they receive if they perform well?

- Is the reward system permanent, or will it be modified or discontinued once strategic initiatives are fully implemented?

- Will everyone be eligible for rewards? For example, if the reward system involves bonuses for the sale of a new product, will it be just for those in product development, those in sales, or both?

Rewarding Results – Part 2

New companies/start-ups may not have the ability to open their coffers and provide excessive, or even competitive, financial (extrinsic) rewards to employees. However, it's important to not overlook the other types of personal (intrinsic) rewards that can be very attractive to many talented employees.

- **Recognition**: earning praise from peers and/or supervisors; having the ability to speak about accomplishments in front of others, or share a creative approach that's been developed.

- **Intellectual challenges**: The opportunity to work on mentally demanding/engaging projects.

- **Power and influence**: Ability to make important decisions; participate in major strategy decisions.

- **Affiliation**: Working with co-workers who share similar skills, interests and ideologies.

- **Managing people**: Responsibility for directing other's efforts and/or projects.

- **Positioning/Mentorship**: Gaining access to experience and/or contacts who will advance career prospects.

- **Lifestyle**: Time to pursue other interest in life (i.e. personal days, flex schedules, telecommuting, etc.)

'The supreme quality for leadership is unquestionably integrity. Without it, no real success is possible, no matter whether it is on a section gang, a football field, in an army, or in an office."

- *Dwight D. Eisenhower*

"Don't find fault, find a remedy."

– Henry Ford

Brainstorming

In 1999, Amaani Lyle, a writer's assistant on the popular NBC TV show "Friends" filed as sexual harassment lawsuit claiming that in the show's writer's room, writers and producers regularly used "sexually coarse, vulgar, and demeaning language in the workplace." Warner Brothers, the parent company of NBC, argued that the writer's room was a special, unique place – "a creative environment" that required writers' to speak freely as "a part of the creative process that helps to develop better scripts."

The California Supreme Court, in a 7-0 decision, rejected Lyle's harassment suit and sided with Warner Brothers and NBC. If you are reading this, and you work in Film/TV production, congratulations – problem solved! But what about the rest of us? What lessons can we take away from this issue?

1. Under no circumstances allow racially/sexually/religiously demeaning language, etc. to occur in your workplace. Your lawsuit will not turn out as well.

2. "Brainstorming" does require freedom. You must create an environment where your employees are given the latitude to discuss every aspect of a problem, without restriction. Encourage respectful creativity!

3. "Brainstorming" is **not** agenda-driven. Too often, leaders seek to have others brainstorm to solve a specific problem (that is your job). Instead, it should be used to invite others to express new creative avenues, concepts and ideas for the organization.

Language of Leadership

You've probably heard the phrase, "The more things change, the more they stay the same." While this might not be true for every aspect of life, there is some substantial merit in regards to how leaders communicate with, and persuade, others. Compelling leaders are often called upon to persuade people to undertake tasks or make great changes under very uncertain circumstances. In ancient Greece and Rome, there was a basic, immutable concept: *persuasion is a result of the words spoken to the listener and the style/style in which they are delivered*

With all of our current technology and mediated forms of communication, this idea has often been forgotten. However, you must master this basic fundamental. Would you try and build a house without first understanding how to use a hammer? Fortunately, the ancient rhetorician, Aristotle, has provided us with three specific "language types" that are integral to effective communication and persuasion.

Logos: The ability to read situations correctly using objective data, information, etc. The ability to persuade/motivate by using information and arguments based on standardized, universally-agreed upon information.

Ethos: Authentic language and credibility. The ability to express values, hopes, desires in a credible way. Language that creates a sense of commitment and trust.

Pathos: The ability to utilize emotion. Developing a sense of empathy. Learning to listen, engage and truly be "emotionally present" in dealing with employees and customers/clients.

Listening

If you have children, especially teenagers, already know there is a difference between hearing and listening. "Hearing" is physiological, while "listening" is psychological/emotional. Effective leadership cannot happen without effective listening. It involves understanding what is being said, and more importantly, what is not being said.

If you've ever been blindsided by a valuable employee quitting and taking another job, think back....they most likely made clear statements about their dissatisfaction. Yes, you heard them, but you didn't listen. So, how can you become a more effective listener?

Attention: Be mindful. Consciously remove distractions. Be present in face-to-face communication. Stay engaged.

Ask Questions: Clarify when uncertain. Don't assume or try to "interpret" what the speaker is saying. Engage in the discussion.

Don't Interrupt: Do your best to avoid correcting/judging. Listen completely all the way through first. By interrupting you may change the direction of the conversation and miss information that could have been expressed.

Watch body language: Are they leaning close or away? Arms crossed? Shuffling feet? Avoiding eye contact? 65-70% of communication is expressed nonverbally. Don't miss 65-70% of the conversation.

Finding "Needs"

Whether you are dealing with employees, clients, or competitors – they all have needs. How can you be sure of this? Because they're human. The influential humanistic psychologist Abraham Maslow (1908-1970) developed his theory of needs based on the premise that individuals seek to have "peak experiences" in their life and innately seek to reach their ultimate potential. "Maslow's Hierarchy" gives you an excellent template to help guide your leadership actions, and proposals, to fulfill the needs of those that you're trying to influence/lead. Each need area is a particular target that you can use to strongly focus your actions to achieve your end goal.

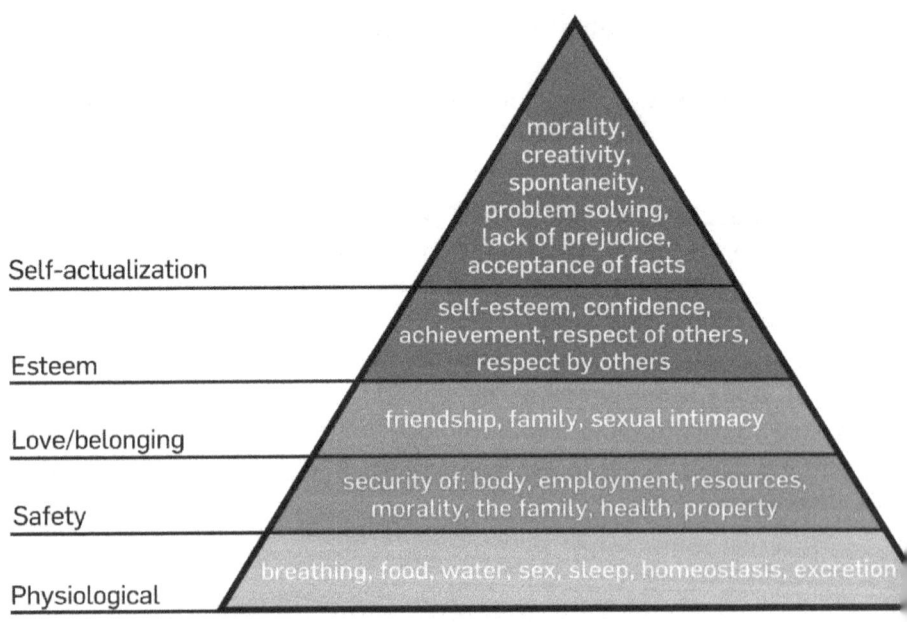

Making Sense and Sharing Sense

Communication, especially for leaders, is all about "making sense" to their respective audience. The process of communication is about *making sense* out of the world and *sharing that sense with others* via created symbols (i.e. thoughts, concepts, objects, language). We "make sense" through verbal and nonverbal messages. No matter what form of communication you engage in, there are some key components involved.

Source: The originator of the idea/message.

Message: The information being communicated by the source.

Encoding: Putting the idea/message into a form that can be interpreted (language, symbols, etc.)

Channel: The means through which the idea/message is sent.

Decoding: The receiver of the idea/message interprets it.

Feedback: The response of the receiver to the idea/message.

"One does not plan and then try to make circumstances fit those plans. One tries to make the plans fit the circumstances."

– George S. Patton, Jr.

"The task of the leader is to get their people from where they are to where they have not been."

– Henry Kissinger

Defining the Business

When I worked at New Line Cinema, I worked with "creative" types (i.e. actors and directors) and "analytical" types (i.e. international finance and accounting). Both were trying to accomplish the same "defining" goal of the company: to produce movies that turn a profit. Therefore, clearly defining your business or organization is imperative to future success. If you can't define who you are or what you do, how can you expect customers or clients to define it?
The equation is deceptively simple:

> Clear definition = understanding = sales

Developing a good business definition should take into account the following factors:

1) Customer needs, or *what* is being satisfied.

2) Customer groups, or *who* is being satisfied.

3) Technologies and/or functions performed, or *how* customer needs are satisfied.

While defining your business is not always easy or obvious, it is the foundational bedrock on which everything rests. First, because it enables you to clearly define/manage your goals. Second, it gives your customers a clear identity that they can attach to your business. Third, it will better enable you differentiate yourself from the competition.

The "Five Point" Leader

Leaders are called upon to handle short-term issues, long-term issues, interpersonal conflict, finances, etc. This can quite easily lead to being overwhelmed. Furthermore, far too many "leadership" books are either too specific or are filled with information that is not applicable to the real world and cannot be utilized quickly. This book, I hope you're finding, is a remedy to that.

So, in keeping with that spirit, I'd like to suggest you develop a leadership plan, more specifically, a plan is designed to keep you on track by managing the five components/responsibilities of an effective manager or leader.

1) **Strategic vision:** create a sense of purpose for the organization, infused with long-term direction and a clear mission.

2) **Conversion:** Turning the strategic vision and mission into measurable objectives and performance targets.

3) **Craftsmanship:** Developing a strategy to achieve the results desired.

4) **Engagement:** Implementing and executing the strategy as efficiently and effectively as possible.

5) **Evaluation:** Reviewing new developments and opportunities. Adjusting long-term plans/objectives as needed.

Too Many Cooks

Gaius Cornelius Tactius (56 AD- 120 AD) was one of the most well-respected historians of ancient Rome. His work is still an influential source for academics, literature scholars and historians of today. Perhaps you're familiar with his phrase, "This is an unfair thing about war; victory is claimed by all, failure to one." Sound familiar? In 1961, after the failed "Bay of Pigs" invasion, President John F. Kennedy stated, "Victory has 100 fathers and defeat is an orphan."

As a leader, you will often get too much credit for success, and all the blame when things go bad. Sounds fun, right? However, no leader operates in a vacuum, and you still need to rely on the right "cooks" to help shape policy and provide insight. Who should you look for so that you don't invite the wrong people or have "too many cooks" in your kitchen?

Information Providers: Leaders/managers of respective departments (sales, development, advertising) that can inform, educate, update others about the progress in their respective departments.

Advice/External Sources: Those that have current or past experience in a particular discipline or industry. They can often provide unique insights from outside your company and be a reservoir of experience, trends, historical narratives, business culture, etc.

Specialized Expertise: Those with a particular, specific skill-set. Can be from inside or outside the company, but can often be utilized to facilitate meeting and development projects.

Authorization: Those who might be required to sign-off or approve any decisions made. Often required in the case of financial or contract decisions.

Work-Life Balance

Many people believe that the concept of "work-life balance" is a post Generation-X or "New Millennial" creation. However, the "work-leisure" dichotomy was first developed in the 1800s and arose as a result of increasing industrialization and the exodus of workers from outlying, agrarian regions into growing cities. As people began to work in locations that were different from where they lived- two separate worlds developed, each with their benefits and deficits. The official terminology of "work-life balance" came into vogue in the United Kingdom in 1970 and was introduced to the United States in 1986.

Leaders, especially entrepreneurs, are often advised to be obsessed, relentless, consumed, laser-focused, etc. They're told to "eat, live and breathe" their company or start-up. This "advice" is hogwash. Seriously, how are you going to create a new social media app or a business that people love, if you're not out with **actual people**? The same ones who might want your product or service, right? Every time I've struggled professionally, it was because my personal/domestic life was in turmoil – and vice versa. Inevitably, in one area or the other - I was obsessed, relentless, consumed. The result? I was personally miserable and my work was miserable!

Get a hobby. Work out. Learn a second language. Join a sports league. Volunteer. Take a cooking class. Find something, **anything** outside of your business/profession that emotionally, physically, intellectually or socially nourishes you. You will be a stronger, sharper and a better leader.

Guaranteed.

"The first responsibility of a leader is to define reality. The last is to say thank you. In between, the leader is a servant."

-Max DePree

"Before you are a leader, success is all about growing yourself. When you become a leader, success is all about growing others."

-Jack Welch

Social Loafing

Social loafing is a phenomenon that occurs when groups are tasked to complete a goal. In this instance, one or more members of the group are content to stay back and let others do the work, carry the group, etc. However, not all of the motivations for this are malicious or intentional, yet they are often associated with the following attitudes and/or conditions:

- The group is too big. I feel my contributions are unnecessary and/or valueless.

- I'm in competition with co-workers, and I'd like to see them fail/lose.

- I will get the ultimate benefits, regardless of participation, so why bother?

- I'm afraid I can't contribute and I doubt my competence.

- I'm very anxious being in a group environment.

- I don't buy into/support the goals of the group.

- I'm preserving my autonomy.

Systems of Organizational Control

No matter what organization you're involved in, at the very root, there is a system of control. A variety of organizational theorists have attempted to explain these (with various levels of success), yet U.S. political scientist Richard Edwards has specified three "root" systems that are well worth noting.

Simple: Based on relationships that are direct and personal, but can also be arbitrary (i.e. small businesses with a direct owner/operator, independent business with no other offices, regions, etc.) In this system, the owner can/usually gives direct orders to employees.

Technical: Relies on the technology of the organization to manage employees' work and physical bodies (i.e. assembly line, CSR call-centers, etc.)

Bureaucratic: Built on a system of rules, regulations, norms, and habits. (i.e. dress, lunch breaks, management, production goals, corporate training, etc.)

In the last several years, there has been a movement away from codified, obtrusive means of organizational control to more subtle ones. This is in no small part due to rapid change (at least by industry/economic standards) from a "production" economy to an "information" economy. However, despite this shift, organizational control systems will always play a role, because leaders of organizations will always be dealing with human employees.

The Only Constant? Change

Changes in an organization are 99.999% guaranteed to happen at some point. If you've never experienced it yet, you're either a new start-up or you're fixing to go out of business, because you didn't adjust to market/consumer demands. So, what are some of the "types" of change and what are their causes?

Intentionality: Direct response to external pressures. These are deliberate, conscious and planned –such as changing a company name, or attempting to broaden the scope of the business.

Timing: Can either be a result of abrupt, short-term goals or a more gradual, evolutionary re-positioning of the organization. (i.e. immediate layoffs vs. annual market surveys to identify opportunities for growth or improvement).

Impetus: Change can be initiated *externally* (new regulations), *internally* (CEO wanting to change the vision of the company), *centrally* (management and strategic planning), and *non-centrally* (through experimentation and innovation by employees).

Popularity: Based on how stakeholders, employees, etc. view the change initiatives. If the change is considered particularly radical, leaders will need to allot extra time to influencing/persuading.

Control: Focuses on how change is implemented, which will be either – programmed (i.e. "top-down," from management) or adaptive (i.e. "bottom-up," initiated at varying levels of the organization.)

Leadership and Argumentation

Human beings, by evolutionary nature, are afraid of argumentation. Very often, even when we hear the word "argument" we immediately paint a less than pleasant mental picture. Effective "Argumentation," however, is integral to a well-functioning organization. From upper management to lower-level employees, argumentation is occurring on a daily basis. There are four fundamental types of appeals, or "lines of argument."

Heart: Designed to appeal to emotions and/or feelings. Can lead to manipulation and unwise judgments. Can sometimes be very valid, but can also be ploys to win attention, consent, or sympathy.

Values: Closely related to emotional appeals, but are designed to work within specific groups of people (i.e. age, class, gender). Fundamentally look to (1) ask others to live up to traditions, higher principles, etc. (2) complain that the group has not done so, or has fallen short of those traditions or principles.

Character: An appeal to ethos (ethics). An argument based from seeming honest, wise, trustworthy, etc. Seeks to develop authority in an organic, subtle manner.

Facts and Reason: Based on finding correct linkages between claims and supporting reasoning. Heavily supported by tangible evidence and past experience. Driven by quantifiable data and information.

A Quaker put up on a vacant piece of land next to his home: THIS LAND WILL BE GIVEN TO ANYONE WHO IS TRULY SATISFIED. A wealthy farmer, who was passing by, read the sign and said to himself, "Since our friend the Quaker is so ready to part with this land, I might as well claim it before someone else does. I am a rich man and have all I need, so I certainly qualify."

With that, he went up to the door and explained what he was there for the land. The Quaker asked him, "And are you truly satisfied?" The man responded, "Yes. I am indeed, for I have everything I need." The Quaker responded, "Well, if you are satisfied, what do you want the land for?"

Epilogue

Leadership, and by extension, managing people is an inexact science. The variables are endless and the challengers are numerous and ever-changing. However, if you can have a firm foundation and understanding of some principles of leadership, you can be well on your way to finding your own personal leadership style and "management voice." No book has every answer to the question of leadership or can provide absolute, fail-safe solutions. Be wary of authors or consultants who tout a particular "system" or claim to have a silver bullet to solve all your leadership and management problems.

In this book, I have endeavored not to provide a system, but to expose you to a wide variety of concepts, theories, quotes, anecdotes that I believe, each in their own way, provide very potent insights into the world of leadership. It is my hope that this text has served you in providing a good starting point for your journey to leadership excellence and success.

Sincerely,

Eric Dunning, Ph.D.

Bibliography

Balzac, Stephen. *Organizational Development*. McGraw-Hill, 2011.

Beebe, Steven and Timothy Mottet. *Business and Professional Communication*. Pearson, 2013

Bennis, Warren and Joan Goldsmith. *Learning to Lead*. Perseus, 2010.

Berton, Pierre. *The lost interview: Bruce Lee: The Pierre Berton Show, 9 December 1971*. Place of publication not identified: BN Publishing, 2009.

Canfield, Jack, et al. *The Power of Focus*. HCI, 2000.

Cheney, George, et al. *Organizational Communication in an Age of Globalization*. Waveland, 2010

Fisher, Roger and William Ury. *Getting to Yes*. Penguin, 2nd ed. 1991

Grant, Michael. *Greek and Latin authors, 800 B.C.-A.D. 1000*. New York: H.W. Wilson Co., 1980.

Harvard Business Press. *Executing Strategy*. Harvard Press, 2009

Heller, Robert. *Achieving excellence*. DK Publishing, 1999.

McGregor, Douglas, and Joel E. Cutcher-Gershenfeld. *The human side of enterprise*. Place of publication not identified: McGraw-Hill Professional, 2008.

Mure, G. R. G. *Aristotle*. Whitefish, MT: Kessinger Pub., 2010.

Pondy, Louis R., Dale E. Fitzgibbons, and John A. Wagner. *Organizational power and conflict: a bibliography*. Monticello, IL: Vance Bibliographies, 1980.

Thompson, Arthur and A.J. Strickland. *Crafting and Implementing Strategy*. Irwin Press, 1995

Notes

Notes

Notes